Led by His Spirit

Spoken through Poems

Stephanie R. Miller

5 Fold Media
Visit us at www.5foldmedia.com

Led by His Spirit: Spoken through Poems
Copyright © 2013 by Stephanie R. Miller
Published by 5 Fold Media, LLC
www.5foldmedia.com

All rights reserved. No part of this book may be reproduced, stored in a retrieval system, or transmitted in any form or by any means—electronic, mechanical, photocopy, recording, or otherwise—without prior written permission of the copyright owner, except by a reviewer who wishes to quote brief passages in connection with a review for inclusion in a magazine, website, newspaper, podcast, or broadcast. Cover imagery copyright kevron2001 and n_eri-Fotolia.com. The views and opinions expressed from the writer are not necessarily those of 5 Fold Media, LLC.

Scripture quotations are taken from the New American Standard Bible®, Copyright © 1960, 1962, 1963, 1968, 1971, 1972, 1973, 1975, 1977, 1995 by The Lockman Foundation. Used by permission.

ISBN: 978-1-936578-70-2
Library of Congress Control Number: 2013942094

Contents

Introduction	5
Titus 2, Where Are You?	6
The Spirit of Superwoman	9
Undeniably Him ✻ To be read	11
Joy for Your Journey	13
A Winning Witness	15
A Purposeful Plight	17
A Truth Serum	19
A Lifestyle of Transgression	21
Sweatless Victory	22
A Dark, Yet Desperate, Deliverance	24
Eyes to See	26
A Disease with Depth	28
A Wall of Fire	29
Lies in Your Eyes	30
✻ Pillow Prayers	31
The Ultimate Fret	33
The Spirit of Peninnah in You	35
A Message to Manny	37
A Gift in the Storm	39
20 New Direction	41
Entangled	43
Calling	45
Twelve	46
A Just Cause	48
Self-Idolatry	50
A Cleansing Rain	52
Preparation of the Kingdom	53

A Critical Consecration	55
Consecration through Obedience	57
I Declare	58
A Blind Walk	60
Choose Ye This Day	62
The Downfall of Looking for People	63
My Declaration to Thee	65
An Empty Reach	67
In Spite of What I Feel	69
A Healthy Affliction	71
The Revealing	72
Slow to Speak	74
The Butterfly Effect	75
A Severing of Souls	77
Discretion	79
Idolatry's Intrusion	81
Be Free in Jesus' Name	83
Know that I am God	85
The End of My Wilderness Experience	86
An Anointed Return	88
Beyond Numbers	90
Where is Anna?	91
Forty Years Full	92
A New Land	94
About the Author	97

Introduction

This book was written both introspectively and retrospectively. Many of my trials occurred prior to the impartation of these poetic messages, yet God used these writings to detail my wilderness experience and His divine design for my healing and deliverance. My promised land was full of everything I needed to walk in purpose. However, my will, ideas, plans, bitterness, unforgiveness, pride, and fear had to die in the wilderness! True restoration rests in the hands of our Master.

This collection was birthed from quiet intimacy with God. As I worshipped, prayed, or read His holy Word, He produced each message. These words were sent when I needed instruction, or reassurance that He had not forgotten me. As you read each poem, I pray that you will be encouraged to stand still and know that He is God!

> "Now to Him who is able to do far more abundantly beyond all that we ask or think, according to the power that works within us, to Him be the glory in the church and in Christ Jesus to all generations forever and ever. Amen" (Ephesians 3:20-21).

> "Cease striving and know that I am God; I will be exalted among the nations, I will be exalted in the earth" (Psalm 46:10).

Led by His Spirit: Spoken through Poems

Exactly seven days after one of our visits to Cincinnati, Ohio, this poem was birthed. My husband, Kevin, and I had visited his nephew's church for the first time. God spoke to us through the bishop of their congregation. One of the many things he said to me was, "Your relationship with God is going to change. It's going to be just you and God. Everything is going to change." This was the beginning of my new journey with Him.

> "Older women likewise are to be reverent in their behavior, not malicious gossips nor enslaved to much wine, teaching what is good, so that they may encourage the young women to love their husbands, to love their children, to be sensible, pure, workers at home, kind, being subject to their own husbands, so that the word of God will not be dishonored" (Titus 2:3-5).

Titus 2, Where Are You?

Again, I lie here on the floor
Feeling as if I can take no more.
Prostrate before my precious Lord,
Calling His name to fill this void—
The void I thought my marriage would fill
Only to find that I was still
Alone in this office as a wife,
Full of silent pain and strife.

I'd searched for "her" for many years,
To help me dry this stream of tears,
But she never came to rescue me
'Cause the depth of my pain she could not see.

Stephanie R. Miller

She'd been called to walk me through this pain
But in this place she'd allowed me to remain.
Oblivious to my need for prayer
My Titus 2 Woman didn't seem to care.
Not enough to lie on her face to seek Thee,
And ask You how she might support me.
Instead she'd only look from a distance—
Perhaps she assumed she'd meet resistance.

But God you told her to teach me how to love him and nurture my baby—
It just requires an unselfish and compassionate lady
To lay down the burdens of her own life
By standing in the gap for another's wife.
So, I've come to remind my sisters and mothers of God
To remember the road on which you've already trod.
It's a safe place for your sister or daughter to walk;
She is begging you to share, pray, or simply talk.

No woman can honor her vows alone—feeling heavy, overwhelmed, and bound
'Cause nobody's come to save her from her thoughts, emotions, and sinking ground.
Yes, only GOD can deliver our heavy-burdened souls,
But He needs the women of God to walk in their respective roles.

As God blesses you to celebrate many years of matrimony,
Daughters and sisters in Christ need to hear your REAL testimony!

Led by His Spirit: Spoken through Poems

It will teach younger women to stand and go through!

They just need a godly example from you.

Titus 2 Woman, where are you? Help us by allowing us to walk with you.

Stephanie R. Miller

There was a season when I endured physical symptoms without a medical diagnosis. Extreme light-headedness rendered me bedridden. However, it became evident that God needed to minister to me alone. As I interceded for the women around me, I heard these words: "The Spirit of Superwoman." The Lord led me to the book of Ephesians to further understand His meaning behind this poem.

> "Therefore, take up the full armor of God, so that you will be able to resist in the evil day, and having done everything, to stand firm. Stand firm therefore, having girded your loins with truth, and having put on the breastplate of righteousness, and having shod your feet with the preparation of the gospel of peace; in addition to all, taking up the shield of faith with which you will be able to extinguish all the flaming arrows of the evil one. And take the helmet of salvation, and the sword of the Spirit, which is the word of God" (Ephesians 6:13-17).

The Spirit of Superwoman

The spirit of Superwoman is not a figment of our imagination,
Not a cartoon character, but a necessary realization.

It's a clear reflection of you and me,
Standing exactly where He assigned us to be.

A reflection of undeniable strength in Him,
It's our boldness in Christ, birthed from within.

It's an embrace of God's power, His strength, His might.
It's the way He sees us as we fight this fight.

Led by His Spirit: Spoken through Poems

If we relinquish our wills, our thoughts and old pain,
Imagine how He'd use us to prove that He reigns!
Imagine how liberating our fellowship would become—
Denying ourselves and binding together as one.
The spirit of Superwoman is empowerment from above
To navigate the earth realm using God's divine love.

Stephanie R. Miller

The following day, I was still confined to my bed. The poetry shifted drastically. This was the day when the Holy Spirit began to speak *to* me *through* me.

> "Behold, I stand at the door and knock; if anyone hears My voice and opens the door, I will come in to him and will dine with him, and he with Me" (Revelation 3:20).

Undeniably Him

Three in the morning He calls forth to me—
His nudging I sense as I rest quietly.

Enter into My presence, My child, hear Me now.
I need to use your voice, and only I can show you how.

Speak through My writings as I expose your loss and gain.
Only I can offer you comfort as you release unbearable pain.

The degree to which I've called you will explain some earthly mess.
My child, understand this has only been a test.

I look to find obedience as you stumble, struggle, and win.
I've hidden you for so long and I will again and again.

Don't seek man's approval as I test you with fire.
Endurance is the proving ground I ultimately desire.

Led by His Spirit: Spoken through Poems

Give your life back to Me and I'll demonstrate My will.
You'll witness My deliverance as you remain still.

I call you in the morning while your family's at rest.
I know you very dearly, and it's when you listen best.

Pain and frustration distanced me from the presence of the Lord. I made carnal decisions and listened to the thoughts and opinions of others. I sought things that appeared to make me "happy," but every "happy" experience was short-lived. I didn't realize that I truly needed something more powerful than my circumstances and my thoughts. I would soon learn that there was a distinct difference between happiness and joy. My life had been filled with overlapping seasons of happiness and pain. Yet, it wasn't until I experienced the joy of the Lord that I learned to walk in its power.

> "Do not be grieved, for the joy of the Lord is your strength" (Nehemiah 8:10b).

Joy for Your Journey

Joy extends beyond being happy,
Its origin is from our Father above.
It's birthed from His covenant with us—
A reflection of unconditional love.

It's powerful enough to strengthen you
Through that which encumbers you most.
It sustains your very thinking,
Enabling you to remain close

Enough to hear Him minister—
A peace too complex for your mind to grasp.
It reaches the depth of your spirit
To uplift, encourage, and surpass

Led by His Spirit: Spoken through Poems

The overwhelming circumstances of this life
By igniting a spiritual flame.
The burning sensation of this fire
Creates an urgency to call on His name.

When you call upon the name of Jesus,
The spirit of joy resonates in your heart.
There's an insatiable desire to praise Him
For the manifestation of His part.

He superseded our meager attempts
To create "happy thoughts" and "happy days"
By imparting the spirit of joy
To encourage us to embrace His ways.

Stephanie R. Miller

To witness is to share God's goodness, grace, and mercy from the perspective of your own personal lens. This poem encouraged me to reach into the lives of those around me by transferring His love. It was also a call to be free to witness in both professional and personal settings. It was time to reveal the depth of what God had done for me.

> "'You are My witnesses,' declares the Lord, 'And My servant whom I have chosen, so that you may know and believe Me and understand that I am He. Before Me there was no God formed, and there will be none after Me. I, even I, am the Lord, and there is no savior besides Me'" (Isaiah 43:10-11).

A Winning Witness

Be My witness in the days to come—
Totally dependent upon the Holy One.
Leave all your burdens and cares at My feet.
Keep your mind on My purpose and soon you will reap
The seeds you have sown are neither scattered nor lost.
I know that you've labored and paid a high cost.

But rest assured, My child, that I've kept you all along,
Hiding you close as you worshipped in song.
Dear child, I heard you as you cried out in pain,
But no hindrance shall stop this upcoming rain.
I'll shower you with favor and gifts from above—
Overwhelming expressions of My unfailing love.

Led by His Spirit: Spoken through Poems

Be My witness as you labor in schools and at home.
Testify of My goodness and how you've overcome.
Don't hesitate to share the depth of your despair,
For someone lives in anguish and needs to know that I'm there.

Please keep your words simple, but confident, nonetheless.
Tell your story, My dear child, release and confess!
Proclaim with joy the comfort you've found in My Spirit.
Declare it with power, My child, they must hear it!
Be My witness on this earth, sharing your faith as you speak.
It's your witness that will draw them from the life of sin they seek.

As we work, our service is ultimately unto the Lord. When we take credit for His marvelous work through us, we minimize the impact that He's able to have in the area of business. In His infinite wisdom, God patterns our work experiences for His purpose and plan. Each experience equips us with a natural skill or affords us a spiritual pruning.

> "Let your light shine before men in such a way that they may see your good works, and glorify your Father who is in heaven" (Matthew 5:16).

A Purposeful Plight

God's purpose isn't focused on the grandiose things you do,
Especially when the accolades ultimately return to you.

His purpose doesn't spur you to be a boastful or self-absorbed dependent.
He deserves all the glory; that's why He seeks out a remnant—

A few humble soldiers who will represent His kingdom;
A few obedient servants who will graciously embrace His freedom.

A freedom that offers privileges that extend beyond what you'd ever ask or think;
A freedom that supersedes opinions that would potentially shift your life out of sync.

So I'm embracing His call to servanthood as I continue with Premier Designs—
I'm embracing His unique love for me as He chastens, encourages, and refines.

However God blesses my business, I'll serve Him with my heart, soul, and might.

I'm compelled to remember that it's *His* purpose that propels my plight.

Stephanie R. Miller

One of the most powerful strongholds that entrapped me was lies. The absence of truth limited my vision, peace, relationships, purpose, and freedom. I had been given the Holy Spirit to lead and guide me in all truth, but fear negated its power in my life.

> "And you will know the truth, and the truth will make you free" (John 8:32).

A Truth Serum

The Holy Spirit is a truth serum that rushes through your veins,
Exposing every hidden place
Until nothing else remains.

No secret ever lingers, no story goes untold,
For the nature of His Spirit
Is to ultimately unfold.

The stirring of the Holy Spirit will prompt you to follow His lead.
It will never overwhelm you,
But simply plant a seed.

The seed urges you to listen, and sometimes act in faith.
Frequently the seed reminds you
That you merely have to wait.

Be patient as He ushers you into the realm of truth.
The seed that He has planted

Will eventually bear fruit.
The fruit must fully ripen before you're allowed to eat.
It must reach full maturity
So its purpose will be complete.

The blessing of God's truth serum could never be bought or earned.
He imparts His Spirit to His children
So that no stone is left unturned.

Stephanie R. Miller

As I continued to approach my holy God with my carnal ways, I discovered that I was laboring in vain. Oftentimes, I abused His mercy and offended Him with my words and deeds. Regardless of the offense, I sinned against God and God alone.

> "'Therefore, I will judge you, O house of Israel, each according to his conduct,' declares the Lord God. 'Repent and turn away from all your transgressions, so that iniquity may not become a stumbling block to you'" (Ezekiel 18:30).

A Lifestyle of Transgression

Forgive us, dear Lord, for the lifestyles we lead!
We squander time and money while neglecting our spiritual needs.

We abuse Your gift of mercy as we transgress again and again.
We've embraced our way of doing things, complacent with familiar sin.

Do we seek Your direction as we anxiously move to and fro?
Do we consciously abandon Your wisdom as it urges us to grow?

YES!

Conviction hearkens our ears to escape our fleshly ways,
But we've fallen in love with carnality, hindering a lifestyle of praise.

"Sweatless victory" was a phrase that my sister-in-Christ, Barbara, would use as she awaited God's hand to move. She was confident in His word and trusted Him to supply her needs. This poem was written to encourage her.

> "And that all this assembly may know that the Lord does not deliver by sword or by spear; for the battle is the Lord's and He will give you into our hands" (I Samuel 17:47).

Sweatless Victory

Sweatless victory
Through insurmountable pain.

Sweatless victory
To exemplify My reign.

Sweatless victory
To minimize troubling thoughts.

Sweatless victory
Encouraging you to do as you ought.

Sweatless victory
Over your financial woes.

Sweatless victory
Over seething attacks from your foes.

Stephanie R. Miller

Sweatless victory
To validate your position.

Sweatless victory
To a place of transition.

Sweatless victory
Through no effort of your own.

Sweatless victory
Protects the power of My throne.

Led by His Spirit: Spoken through Poems

One night as I prayed for a dear friend, the depth of intercession became painful and tearful. God spoke these words regarding her condition.

> "And do not lead us into temptation, but deliver us from evil. For Yours is the kingdom and the power and the glory forever. Amen" (Matthew 6:13).

A Dark, Yet Desperate, Deliverance

(A Poem of Intercession)

Move, child, from these haunting and taunting dark places
Which create images of strange and unkind faces

Lamenting in shadows of past fear and shame,
Hiding in closets of mistrust and blame.

Come forth to My light as I unleash these shackles;
Escape the dungeon where you, by Satan, were tackled.

Experience My luminous and glorious path!
The one I predestined before you succumbed to Satan's wrath.

Shout from the depths of your womb to My ear.
Relinquish your will and overwhelming fear.

Tamper no more with that which poisons you—
Arise as My vessel, empty, fresh, and renewed!

Stephanie R. Miller

In My Spirit you have liberty, for Christ set you free!
You are My workmanship, designed to worship Me.

Led by His Spirit: Spoken through Poems

As believers, God equips us with "double vision" —we have the natural ability to see the daily occurrences in our midst, but we also have a spiritual vision which enables us to see what lies beneath actions, words, and situations. God trusted me enough to begin to confirm what I believed I was seeing.

> "For to us God revealed them through the Spirit; for
> the Spirit searches all things, even the depths of God"
> (I Corinthians 2:10).

Eyes to See

Just as Jesus spat on the soil and caused a man to see,
I am washing your vision, child, in order to set you free.

No more pain and wonder causing a life of torment;
You'll understand the darkness and why you have been sent.

Sent with a fresh anointing to uplift, encourage, and reveal
The hidden, ugly places that have strategically been concealed.

Don't view this as a curse or a life lived in shame.
Agree with this deliverance and pray in Jesus' name.

Align yourself with My Word and understand that the time has come—
Every unclean thing must submit to the Sovereign and Holy One.

I will use My writings through you to serve as your guide.
Lie prostrate, fast, and listen—direction I will provide.

Stephanie R. Miller

I've not caused you to suffer in vain, as you believe in your fragile mind;
I've longed for you to draw near to Me and submit to that which is divine.

Eager ears will be your greatest asset as I speak words that you have not heard.
I'm unleashing your ability to see and hear Me so that you will rely solely on My Word.

The wounded, abused, and downtrodden have fallen prey to the torment of others. Many perpetrators have been exposed publicly and/or privately while many continue to lurk in our midst. Yet God will heal and deliver His children.

> "He heals the brokenhearted and binds up their wounds" (Psalm 147:3).

A Disease with Depth

The disease has poisoned many and brought young men to shame.
It's masked behind religion and a perpetual need to claim

The lives of those fatherless victims, falling prey to this deep, dark world—
An underground world of terror that strips men of their God-given worth.

Living lives of isolation and secrecy, as if God has ordained such a powerless walk,
While the inner self suffers silently, they speak confusion and devotion as they talk.

Though God offers ways of escape, their captor has established control.
One has lured these precious men of faith into futile, yet seemingly useful, roles.

God will deliver His children from this sickness so their lives glorify Him.
Dear Lord, we pray for Your sons to transform into upstanding, godly men!

I sensed that we were approaching a difficult season. The Lord continually led me to Scriptures that were indicative of great change. Yet, this poem confirmed God's promise that He would never leave me, nor forsake me.

> "I will never desert you, nor will I ever forsake you"
> (Hebrews 13:5b).

A Wall of Fire

The fire of My Spirit will protect you from the upcoming days of destruction,
Tearing down years of havoc and confusion, but careful to offer specific instruction.

Be quiet in large settings—allow others to talk.
Be confident in My words to you, as they enable you to walk.

My flames will sear the lips of those who speak out against you.
Understand that I'm offering you power to safely pass through.

There will be harsh words to admonish you for your choices and how you've maintained,
Yet My fire will singe strong opinions and protect that which I have sustained.

When your marriage endures this fire, it will burn away the pillars of deceit.
That which remains standing will fill your remaining days with a love that's pure and sweet.

Frequently, I lived as if I didn't see the truth before me, even though I knew that God sent His Holy Spirit as a guide and comfort to me. The ultimate benefit was that He showed me what I needed to see. He then offered a place of refuge to replace the possibility of uncontrolled emotional responses.

> "But when He, the Spirit of truth, comes, He will guide you into all the truth; for He will not speak on His own initiative, but whatever He hears, He will speak; and He will disclose to you what is to come" (John 16:13).

Lies in Your Eyes

Your gaze has changed to a deceptive glance
Revealing the diminishing love and care
For my emotional well-being and spiritual walk—
Your words are empty attempts at flattering talk.

I see that your boldness has grown beyond measure,
Relying on silent and secretive communication.
Disrespectful, sly, and sneaky describe your tainted reputation.

God does not limit the spiritual vision of His children,
He sharpens their discernment and draws them into deeper waters.
In this place there is tranquility and peace within,
Preventing carnal reactions and unforgettable sin.

Praise God for His Spirit that enables me to see
The lies in your eyes that offend your covenant with me!

Stephanie R. Miller

As I trudged through many seasons of depression, I would lie amidst a flood of tears. Sometimes it seemed as if God could not hear or see my pain. I spent countless nights suffering through mental and emotional anguish. I felt abandoned and desperate. It took many years for me to begin to understand how God viewed those nights.

> "For the lamb in the center of the throne will be their shepherd, and will guide them to springs of the water of life; and God will wipe every tear from their eyes" (Revelation 7:17).

Pillow Prayers

My tearstained pillow marks the place of my despair—
A pool of drenched cotton
Coddling my saturated hair.

Doubts, fears, and anger are released in silent streams,
Disturbing restful sleep
And hindering peaceful dreams.

Does God really hear me when I release this silent rain?
As I replay damaging images,
these thoughts inside my brain?

WAIT.

I shall not entertain mental turmoil!
With an anointed, predestined life,

Led by His Spirit: Spoken through Poems

These streams are merely cleansing me
From debilitating strife.

Healing streams of teardrops precede heartfelt worship and prayer.
His presence inhabits my rainstorm and reassures me
Of His promise to be there.

What a sacred, silent, place of intimacy
Between my Father and me.
A liberating exchange of my teardrops
For peaceful refuge in Thee.

Stephanie R. Miller

My need to be in control frequently led me to a place of worry. There were so many circumstances that extended beyond my reach. I loved the Lord, but I hadn't embraced His power. I consistently looked for natural ways to address problems with a deeper spiritual root. On this particular night, I lay awake in my bed, panicking about a financial issue. God's words ministered to my spirit and offered His perspective.

> "And which of you by worrying can add a single hour to his life's span? If then you cannot do even a very little thing, why do you worry about other matters?"
> (Luke 12:25-26).

The Ultimate Fret

When we fret, we make faith a huge anomaly.
It's a picture of panic;
An incurable pathology.

Nerves emitting unnecessary rounds of fire,
Systematically complicating our natural desires.

It's an overreaction to a shift in circumstance.
It's a carnal response that overshadows God's plans.

It's an obsession with control and the need to be right.
It's the essence of the ongoing flesh versus spirit fight.

It's a state of uneasiness that produces complaints,
An outpouring of emotions without restraint.

Yet, its most salient feature is its spontaneous onset—
No preparation needed for the introduction of "fret."

But God offers the solution through His masterful design
By diagnosing situational malignancies as simply "benign."

G od used a women's conference to reconnect me to my dear covenant sister, Elder Sandie. God sent a word of affirmation to me through her. It was the first time that I heard the words "prophetic intercessor." However, these words brought revelation to previous poems and the prophetic undertone that many of them bore. This conference would also bring a greater understanding of the biblical character, Peninnah. The book of Samuel describes her as an antagonistic and bitter woman. Yet, I would soon learn that I, like many other women of faith, carried the "spirit of Peninnah."

> "When the day came that Elkanah sacrificed, he would give portions to Peninnah his wife and to all her sons and her daughters; but to Hannah he would give a double portion, for he loved Hannah, but the Lord had closed her womb. Her rival, however, would provoke her bitterly to irritate her, because the Lord had closed her womb. It happened year after year, as often as she went up to the house of the Lord, she would provoke her; so she wept and would not eat" (I Samuel 1:4-7).

The Spirit of Peninnah in You

Come back, dear daughter, from your cruel and hidden ways;
Disgraceful transgressions against the Ancient of Days.

The spirit of Peninnah has engulfed your very being,
Taking your thoughts captive and erasing God's meaning.

Your subtle Peninnah ways are not evident in the way you walk;
You've learned to mask her using sophisticated talk.

Led by His Spirit: Spoken through Poems

Don't forget to consider Peninnah as she enters your conversation!
She takes pride in how you embrace her while discussing unnecessary information.

Your deep-seated bitterness emits a foul and offensive smell.
I'm your Father and I love you, but your ways I must dispel!

Dear daughter, go forth in freedom and embrace this word I've sent!
Relinquish days and years spent with Peninnah learning to resent.

I've loosed you to do My will on the earth as I say:
The spirit of Peninnah has departed you this hour, this moment, *this day!*

Stephanie R. Miller

My cousin, Patrice, is definitely one of the most fun-loving, humorous, and honest women I know. Since I had previously shared some of my poetry with her, she wanted to know whether or not God had given me any poems about marriage. After our phone conversation, I began to pray and the title of this next poem was deposited in my spirit.

> "So husbands ought also to love their own wives as their own bodies. He who loves his own wife loves himself"
> (Ephesians 5:28).

A Message to Manny

O listen, man of God,
To the words that I will speak!
These words concern your wife
And the life as "one" you seek.

Be gentle with this princess,
My daughter, whom I graciously present.
Be careful with your words,
For a gem to you I've sent.

My son, be My servant
As you bathe her with love and prayers.
Be diligent to always cover her
And minister to her deepest cares.

This marriage you must uphold

In order to represent My throne.
Delight yourself in your wife:
Your personalized precious stone.

Stephanie R. Miller

After a physically and emotionally painful ectopic pregnancy, the Lord filled my womb. Justin Dominick Miller was 8 pounds, 7 ounces, and 21 ½ inches long. As a baby, he enjoyed praise and worship. His spirit brought joy to every day of my life. My darkest days were illuminated by God's light that radiated through our baby boy. He was the perfect gift during many seasons of raging storms.

> "Behold, children are a gift of the Lord, the fruit of the womb is a reward" (Psalm 127:3).

A Gift in the Storm

This babe that you've birthed was My gift to your womb;
No effort of your "labor of love" should you ever assume.

I've granted you this gift and the blessing of his life:
Believe in his purpose and minimize trivial strife.

For the son that you were given was anointed at conception;
His weaknesses don't define his character—it's a matter of perception.

Those with eyes to see know that he's called to do great things;
He'll surpass your imagination as he composes, writes, and sings.

His gift will make room for him as he navigates his call.
I'm with him, leading and guiding, lest he stumble and fall.

Maximize his full potential through spiritual guidance in right and wrong.
Minister to his spirit-man through worship, praise, and song.

Led by His Spirit: Spoken through Poems

My Word will guide his footsteps as he learns to walk closer to Me;
Maturity will usher our relationship into a place of sanctity.

The gift that he's given to you is of love, joy, and laughter.
He's a representation of your future and life hereafter.

His love will be your balance as you pray, watch, listen, and speak.
Understand that his gift will usher you into a greater spiritual seek.

You must be able to lead him in the ways of My word as a believer;
His spirit is open and willing as an available receiver.

Give your best as his mother and teacher, for he trusts the words in your heart.
You're planting seeds of fruitfulness, and establishing a godly start.

The consistency of my prayer life and my desperate reach for God seemed to alert the enemy. There were numerous attacks within our household. The enemy continued to dominate our finances and repeatedly found ways to affect our son and my relationship with my husband. Amazingly, God began to help me identify what was transpiring in the spirit realm, how I contributed, and how I needed to respond.

> "Trust in the Lord with all your heart and do not lean on your own understanding. In all your ways acknowledge Him, and He will make your paths straight" (Proverbs 3:5-6).

New Direction

Dear child, oh hear me, in this prayer to you today:
Forgive all the trouble and pain
That has quickly come your way.

You're fighting against the enemy
That has invaded your godly home.
He's moving to and fro,
Seeking to devour as he roams.

Don't entice him with your tears
And desperate words of insecurity.
Bathe your home with love and prayer,
Cleansing it from ungodly impurities.

Be confident in My words to you
As I speak clearly to you each day.

Led by His Spirit: Spoken through Poems

Abandon your need to control things
As you move into a higher and more spiritual way.

The decisions you make will be crucial
As you raise your son and walk with your husband.
Trust me alone to heal your wounds
And put no confidence in the opinion of man.

Trust your pastor to develop the gifts in you,
As he's been sent to shape and cover a few,
But don't confuse his ability to minister
With the One who's gifted and anointed you.

Have you ever found yourself vacillating between what you believe is true and what you want to be true? That struggle describes many people's lifelong challenges in relationships. Many people find themselves longing for change to such an extent that they will disconnect from their reality. Have you ever found that life was easier and less complicated when you ignored the painful truths associated with your marriage? The challenge for people is to always seek God for answers. As you seek God for direction, He will give you instruction and truth.

> "Be on the alert, stand firm in the faith, act like men, be strong. Let all that you do be done in love"
> (1 Corinthians 16:13-14).

Entangled

Entangled in a web of deceit, lies, and confusion,
Overcome by the enemy's offensive and overbearing intrusion.

An interruption in God's flow and liberty within,
He's pursued God's most precious and lured him into sin.

Be patient with My servant as he stumbles back to My kingdom.
Give him love, kindness, and service, as I usher him back to freedom.

His mind has become weary and his ears no longer hear.
He's succumbed to a rote way of living, driven by fear.

A teacher and worshipper by calling, and divinely anointed to preach,
I'll use your love and forgiveness to counteract any breach.

Don't entangle yourself in this web by denying what you already know.
Live honestly, uprightly, and confidently, allowing My Spirit to flow.

Although I trusted that God was speaking to me, I questioned how each message was both poetic and prophetic in nature. The messages were applicable, timely, specific, and clear. Yet, they were only written by the prompting of the Holy Spirit. I would experience an overwhelming sense of urgency in my spirit as I transcribed what I heard Him say. Frequently, my penmanship was unrecognizable to others as my pen would move faster than I could think. Graciously, He saw fit to explain this "calling" to write.

"My tongue is the pen of a ready writer" (Psalm 45:1b).

Calling

Don't find it queer that I speak to you
In a poetic and prophetic style.
I have need of your voice and ability,
So abandon your selfish guile.

Begin a deeper lifestyle of worship,
Embellished with hours of sincere praise.
Your faith, and ability to hear Me,
I must consistently and diligently raise.

My hand has been set upon you
As a symbol of my power to intervene.
I've placed you in this situation
To pray, obey, and believe.

Shortly after I received the revelation of this call, Elder Sandie contacted me about joining her and several other women in a twelve-week season of consecration and prayer. The request couldn't have been timelier. God was speaking and I heard Him! I simply needed to learn to obey what I heard. We were informed during the first prayer call that the upcoming year was going to realign God's kingdom. It was further explained that "twelve" represented government and law. God also reminded me that my husband and I were in our twelfth year of marriage.

"Restore us to You, O Lord, that we may be restored; renew our days as of old" (Lamentations 5:21).

Twelve

In this twelfth year of marriage
I shall reestablish its worth,

Cleansing it from unrighteousness
And rebuilding its girth.

Don't hesitate to call Me
When its structure is out of order—

I ordained its very existence
And will reseal every border.

Twelve is a number for government
And the establishment of My law;

Stephanie R. Miller

This is the year to change what you're *seeing*
Rather than focus on what you *saw*.

Keep your mind on My Word and promise
Because I will honor what I've said.

Release your pain and frustration
And feast on My daily bread.

Led by His Spirit: Spoken through Poems

Each week, God would give Elder Sandie a specific prayer focus. We would study and pray in order to allow God to minister to us throughout the week. The week would culminate with group intercessory prayer. While reading Psalm 17:1, I identified with David's plea to the Lord. As I kept reading, I sensed God offering me further revelation regarding two words—"just cause."

> "Hear a just cause, O Lord, give heed to my cry; Give ear to my prayer, which is not from deceitful lips" (Psalm 17:1).

A Just Cause

It's for a just cause that I've sent you
To embark upon this endeavor.
It's for a just cause that I saved you
To dwell with Me forever.

It's for a just cause that you've suffered
And endured a most painful death.
It's for a just cause that I've rescued you
To restore, recover, and give you My breath.

Did you ever imagine that I'd hear you
As you searched, wondered, and doubted?
Did you really think that I'd abandoned you
Though you wept, hid, and blatantly shouted?

No, child, I've heard your everyday battle
Against forces you could not control,

Stephanie R. Miller

Struggling to honor your commitment,
Yet unable to fulfill your appointed role.

I sent you glimpses of the truth as you walked with him
Allowing you to begin to see.
But I couldn't offer total revelation
Until your spirit was committed to Me.

This walk with Me is a new adventure
Into the deepest places of the spirit realm.
I'm elevating your worship and prayer life
In small stages, so you won't be overwhelmed.

True intercession is preceded by an inward cleansing from sin and deeply rooted spiritual strongholds. One particular morning, the Lord unveiled the root of my need for control. I heard Him say: "You idolize your opinion. That's why you're so controlling."

> "For through the grace given to me I say to everyone among you not to think more highly of himself than he ought to think; but to think so as to have sound judgment, as God has allotted to each a measure of faith" (Romans 12:3).

Self-Idolatry

Self-idolatry is a debilitating condition—
It resides within your members
And desires to resist transition.

It's impossible to expose without the mind and hand of God
To chasten, renew, and correct
With the power of His holy rod.

You speak words of confidence in your flesh and *not* My Spirit.
It's repulsive and undesirable—
So many refuse to come anywhere near it.

Your tongue is vile and wretched as it speaks words that I have not said.
It utters inconsistencies
Birthed from a spirit that's gone unfed.

Stephanie R. Miller

Humble yourself under My mighty hand and submit only to the words you hear!

Obedience will relieve you of undue stress

And enable your heart to draw near.

As you draw closer to My Spirit and acknowledge the power of My protection

You'll never view yourself in this undeserving way!

You'll simply hearken to My leading and direction.

Led by His Spirit: Spoken through Poems

The Holy Spirit has the ability to cleanse that which infiltrates God's kingdom. God is obligated to protect His investments here on earth. Frequently, it is accomplished through seemingly natural circumstances. This poem describes a forthcoming cleansing of the body of Christ.

> "Therefore, thus says the Lord God, 'I will make a violent wind break out in My wrath. There will also be in My anger a flooding rain and hailstones to consume it in wrath'" (Ezekiel 13:13).

A Cleansing Rain

A rain, a tumultuous rain, is at bay
Preparing to cleanse the indiscretions of this day.

It will destroy all the cobwebs that have lurked in God's kingdom,
Housing the perpetrators who've tormented His people.

This rain will be as powerful as a tsunami's fierce rage.
No generation has witnessed a movement of this stage.

Keep your eyes perched to watch the clouds as they huddle—
The residual will produce a spiritual puddle.

The climate will change as a result of this rain,
And My people will be washed of their insurmountable pain.

Complacency ushers many of us into a haphazard lifestyle. It is a lifestyle that is naturally driven, thus it is in direct opposition to the leading of the Holy Spirit. When we lean on our own understanding, we develop an undeserved confidence in our flesh. My ability to relinquish my thoughts and ways would ultimately establish the groundwork for true obedience and the ability to yield to His plan. This was my preparation for true kingdom living.

> "Trust in the Lord with all your heart and do not lean on your own understanding. In all your ways acknowledge Him, and He will make your paths straight" (Proverbs 3:5-6).

Preparation of the Kingdom

I'm preparing a steadfast and spiritually astute body
That embraces My Spirit and executes My strategy.

No aliens are welcome to this place of consecration and faith.
I'm healing, delivering, and purposing My children through My grace.

Don't fight the work of the kingdom as I prepare your hearts and minds;
You'll witness no other deliverance of this degree, strength, or kind.

I've tired of My people standing in an enormous pit of sin—
Wallowing in their transgressions, refusing to give in.

I've wooed them from the pulpit and chastened them through My Word,
Yet My people have become stiff-necked and ignored all that they've heard.

Led by His Spirit: Spoken through Poems

The consequences will weigh heavily upon My daughters and My sons.
There will be no room for diversion, for I'm coming for each and every one.

Set aside your personal agendas and abandon your pointless routines.
I'm exposing and removing your sin with My spiritual guillotine.

To consecrate is to set aside your time and efforts for the things of God (i.e. worship, prayer, Bible study). During this time of prayer and consecration, I sensed God requiring more of my time and focus. Each morning, I would rise at 4:30 a.m. for prayer and worship. Although I heard His instruction to me, I sensed Him ushering me into a deeper walk. Unfortunately, I did not recognize the seriousness of the call to consecration.

God's instruction was clear, accurate, and necessary. He wanted my mind, soul, body, and spirit to be consecrated unto Him. As our prayer focus required us to conduct self-examinations, God revealed how He wanted me to view this time.

> "For I am the Lord your God. Consecrate yourselves therefore, and be holy, for I am holy" (Leviticus 11:44a).

A Critical Consecration

Consecrate thyself, oh child, to Me and Me alone.

Lay your fleeting and distracting thoughts at the foot of My throne.

I have need of an empty vessel to be used within this region;

A vessel with boldness, and a consecrated heart, to purge every devil, demon, and legion.

Be steadfast on this path that swiftly moves you back and forth!

You've been strengthened to navigate through an extremely unpredictable course.

Don't rely on the strength of your mind or the pain stricken decisions of your heart;

Trust the True Navigator in My Spirit to serve as a compass for your brand new start.

Led by His Spirit: Spoken through Poems

You've not seen this land before, nor have you heard what I must say,
Yet your consecrated spirit and mind will help navigate the way.

True consecration requires a preoccupation with Me and the requests that I impose.
There's a shedding of your old self, so that you thoroughly begin to transpose.

Be thou holy, for I am holy, and I require high standards of you.
There's imminent change on the horizon, and consecration is your only avenue.

I continued to seek the Lord's face each morning, but my struggle mirrored that of Jesus' disciple, Paul. My desires and actions were in direct opposition. God exposed my unhealthy addiction to food! It served as a comfort for pain, frustration, and anger. He gave me instruction to wean me from certain food types and restaurants. Unfortunately, I would succumb to my flesh and fail every time. The difference between this season and many others was that I continued to press forward without condemning myself and abandoning this great seek. Eventually, I walked in victory!

> "All things are lawful for me, but not all things are profitable. All things are lawful for me, but I will not be mastered by anything" (1 Corinthians 6:12).

Consecration through Obedience

To consecrate is to be set aside for the purpose that I desire—
As you obey this call to fast and pray, I'll ignite your spirit with a holy fire.

The fire sustains and assists you with your daily call to tasks.
It will extinguish your need for earthly food without even having to ask.

So don't minimize this call to you, as I've drawn you to this place.
Desire Me more than natural food and I'll begin to fill that space.

Led by His Spirit: Spoken through Poems

As we rapidly approached the end of the year, God began to reveal His plans and gave me very specific instructions. Amazingly, He showed me how the events of my life led to my upcoming year of fulfilled promises and freedom.

> "Therefore, prepare your minds for action, keep sober in spirit, fix your hope completely on the grace to be brought to you at the revelation of Jesus Christ" (1 Peter 1:13).

I Declare

As the sound of this new year begins to permeate the air,
Your God will begin to uplift those who've been distraught or full of despair.

Pull down every stronghold that has saturated the atmosphere;
But you must do it with authority, then begin to stand clear.

For the war that I will rage against the enemy's strategic plans
Will demolish his futile plot through the power of My Almighty hands.

Don't fear this decree, nor doubt My authoritative word.
Set your mind and your spirit on that which you have heard.

Be alert, sober, and vigilant as you enter this new season.
I've outlined your deliverance, and tempered it with My reason.

See, I've brought you out of darkness and into My marvelous light!
I've cured you of depression, and caused demonic forces to take flight.

I've purged you of your insecurities so that your security is wrapped in me.

I've purposed, anointed, and promised you that some day you would be free.

That day is rapidly approaching and My Word will not return void—

Execute with obedience and confidence the instruction that will expose, cleanse, and destroy.

My relationship with my sister is full of love, spontaneity, and strong ties. However, nothing compares to our spontaneous shopping excursions. In the midst of a busy holiday season and my prayer commitment, my sister invited me to visit her in New York. I graciously accepted the offer and enjoyed late night shopping at a local department store, but God would not allow me to abandon Him or the work He was doing through me. While waiting for my return flight, the Lord explained that this journey was actually a walk of faith with a unique purpose.

"For we walk by faith, not by sight" (2 Corinthians 5:7).

A Blind Walk

A blind walk of obedience leads to My ultimate destination.
It's a place of rest, peace, anointing, and restoration.

I've ordained this walk in order to reestablish your faith;
It's erasing past hurt and resetting your pace.

It's a fast forward movement to a place that's unknown;
It's a fashioning of your lifestyle as evidence that you've grown.

Don't tiptoe on this walk,
Move with confidence, grace, and speed.
Learn to obey My voice, and rewards you will receive.

This walk will conquer all of your doubts, fears, and questions.
There's a reassurance that I'm offering under My sacred hand of protection.

Stephanie R. Miller

Each step, I have ordered and purposed just for you.
It's to plant your feet firmly and guide you safely through.

The uncertainty of this walk will correct your spiritual gait;
You'll know exactly when to move and when to stand still and wait.

God had continuously directed me to fast in a specific way. I would soon learn that this struggle would seemingly control me. I could hear the Lord's voice, but I continued to find myself undisciplined and complacent. The seriousness of the call to obey God in this fast became evident.

> "Samuel said, 'Has the Lord as much delight in burnt offerings and sacrifices as in obeying the voice of the Lord? Behold, to obey is better than sacrifice, and to heed than the fat of rams'" (I Samuel 15:22).

Choose Ye This Day

You've breached your reach as you've rapidly approached complacency.
You've heard My voice continually,
Yet you've entered a period of latency.

You don't crave Me as you ought
Because you're blocked by earthly matter—
Disguising spiritual depth by unclear and worthless chatter.

Your mouth speaks unnecessary thoughts
While your heart yearns with sincere desire.
No further will you reach without a true, spiritually-birthed fire.

Stop teasing with your promises and stop wishing from your flesh!
Either you enter this season of consecration,
Or you will suffer from a lack of spiritual depth.

Many years ago, a wise woman of God was ministering at a conference. After she ministered, several of us desired to greet her. As I approached her, she grabbed my hands and said, "Stop running to people. Ask God for what you need."

Recently, the Holy Spirit led me to study 1 Corinthians 3:1-3. The Scripture led me to focus on our carnal need to depend heavily on other people. More specifically, it described our spiritual dependency as those who drink milk or eat solid food. Ultimately, the question was whether or not I was completely weaned from people.

> "It is better to take refuge in the Lord than to trust in man" (Psalm 118:8).

The Downfall of Looking for People

When you begin to seek out people for comfort and/or support,
You're actually seeking for someone to serve as your cohort.

You're in need of something tangible to appease your fleshly desires.
You have need of immediate fulfillment of which you'll soon begin to tire.

For the One that you ultimately need is Our Master and Our King;
He's our Healer, Provider, and Comforter,
The One about Whom we sing.

Don't ever mistake the attention, and short-lived affirmation from imitators,
For the intimacy, passion, and love
Granted by the Alpha and Omega.

Led by His Spirit: Spoken through Poems

He's the Beginning and the End,
Thus His words are without mistake;
He's hastened to supply our needs before the news even breaks.

Count it all joy, dear brothers and sisters,
That we've suffered while He tested and tried us.
For our Father in heaven is the One and Only Comforter
Who has never left or denied us.

Stephanie R. Miller

One year, New Year's Eve arrived and I realized that I was spiritually equipped to cross over into a brand new year. Early that morning, I was led to read Psalm 20. I rejoiced in what I believed God would do and for what He had already done. My spirit began to flood with declarations for that upcoming year!

> "May the Lord answer you in the day of trouble! May the name of the God of Jacob set you securely on high! May He send you help from the sanctuary and support you from Zion! May He remember all your meal offerings and find your burnt offering acceptable! Selah. May He grant you your heart's desire and fulfill all your counsel! We will sing for joy over your victory, and in the name of our God we will set up our banners. May the Lord fulfill all your petitions. Now I know that the Lord saves His anointed; He will answer him from His holy heaven with the saving strength of His right hand. Some boast in chariots and some in horses, but we will boast in the name of the Lord, our God. They have bowed down and fallen, but we have risen and stood upright. Save, O Lord; may the King answer us in the day we call" (Psalm 20:1-9).

My Declaration to Thee

STRENGTHENED beyond tears,
GROWN throughout this year.

HEARING the voice of God,
MATURING under His holy rod.

CONVICTION and clarity given,
RELEASING past areas where I've striven.

Led by His Spirit: Spoken through Poems

BLESSED with the power to stand,
DIRECTED by His almighty hand.

TURNING from the ways of my flesh,
COMPLETE and secure in His breast.

SAFE from my thoughts and my pain,
ANTICIPATING a forthcoming rain.

DETERMINED not to leave this place,
RUNNING until I complete this race.

FIGHTING against the enemy's plans,
PLANTED where my Father says stand.

FRAGILE but determined nonetheless,
BOUND to serve God with my best.

Stephanie R. Miller

I awoke, I prayed, I worshipped, I listened, I cried, I prayed, I worshipped, I listened, I cried. I couldn't hear His voice nor could I sense His presence. I knew that He had not abandoned me because He promised never to leave nor forsake me (Hebrews 13:5). Yet the weight of conviction reminded me of my disobedience. This season required a level of obedience that would surpass even the deepest yearnings of my flesh. I reached until He spoke.

> "And My people who are called by My name humble themselves and pray and seek My face and turn from their wicked ways, then I will hear from heaven, will forgive their sin and will heal their land" (2 Chronicles 7:14).

An Empty Reach

Your hands reach for My presence
And the glory of My weight,
Yet you've consistently dishonored My voice
In order to fill your plate.

To fast is to sacrifice unto Me
The thing that pleases your flesh.
It's an undeniable place of peace,
But a revealing kind of test.

You're reaching for My instruction
And the manna that is your daily bread,
But you've disregarded My warning
And sought refuge in food instead.

Don't deny that which I've provided you
In this precious and secret place.
If you continue to disrespect Me
I'll leave you in the land of disgrace.

FAST!

"Happy Birthday" had a slightly different ring when I celebrated forty-three years of life! Somehow God had forced me to allow myself to acknowledge, state, and understand the depth of my true feelings. A crucial conversation from the previous day afforded me the liberty to connect with my feelings. However, I refused to allow those feelings to dictate my response to people, situations, circumstances, or that which I discerned. In spite of what I felt, this walk would be led solely by the power and authority of God's Holy Spirit.

> "Say to those with anxious heart, 'Take courage, fear not. Behold, your God will come with vengeance; the recompense of God will come, but He will save you" (Isaiah 35:4).

In Spite of What I Feel

In spite of what I feel,
You've watched me shed tears.

In spite of what I feel,
You've abandoned my emotions for years.

In spite of what I feel,
You've imposed both pain and grief.

In spite of what I feel,
You've offered no source of relief.

In spite of what I feel,
You've inflicted years of emotional pain.

Led by His Spirit: Spoken through Poems

In spite of what I feel,
God says my loss is His gain.

Stephanie R. Miller

The book of Job details a remarkable account of one man's faith. Amazingly, Job was afflicted physically and emotionally, yet he refused to curse the name of our God. Similarly, I learned that each natural affliction that I endured bore a spiritual healthiness.

> "It is good for me that I was afflicted, that I may learn Your statutes" (Psalm 119:71).

A Healthy Affliction

Can't explain why He called me to this dry and desert land
Can't explain why He loves me and protects me with His hand

Can't explain why His promises require me to obey
Can't explain why I've chosen to listen and follow His way

For the Father watches over His word to perform that which He's spoken
He's orchestrated unique disasters to repair that which is broken

The depth of what we experience is merely simplistic in the eyes of our Master
He chastens, delivers, and cleanses us to accomplish His purpose a little bit faster

To "reveal" means to uncover that which has been disguised and/or hidden. Revealing sheds new light on someone who has become known as one-dimensional. As a person's spiritual value is truly released, others are blessed by that which was once unknown or unseen. Thus, our ability to see beyond a person's instincts, patterns of sin, insecurities, fears, and strongholds enables us to love without judgment while interceding with sincere conviction.

> "It is He who reveals the profound and hidden things; He knows what is in the darkness, and the light dwells with Him" (Daniel 2:22).

The Revealing

Empty your hands and free your mind,
I'm attempting to give you strategy at this time.

Freedom is imminent for the one that you adore,
For the lifestyle that he's leading is one that I deplore.

Keep him close to your bosom as you pray him out of captivity.
He's yearning for a new lifestyle, yet his fear is masked by insensitivity.

His feelings are numb and his ways have become rote.
Don't be deceived by the external, because he's disguised in this cloak.

This is not how I made him when I formed him in the womb;
He's succumbed to insecurities and now resides inside this tomb.

Stephanie R. Miller

Yet he'll rise, as did your Savior, to see My hand prevail;
No weapon formed against him will keep the true man from being unveiled.

In spite of my profession as a speech-language pathologist, being talkative had become a spiritual, personal, and professional hindrance. This was a season when I needed to strengthen my ability to listen without commenting. On this particular morning, God offered a specific strategy to counteract the enemy's schemes.

> "This you know, my beloved brethren. But everyone must be quick to hear, slow to speak and slow to anger" (James 1:19).

Slow to Speak

Being slow to speak is your weapon
That will confuse the enemy's ways.
It enables you to yield to My instruction
And refrain from carnal responses to what he says.

The tactic is quite simplistic,
As it equips a "talker" like you
To guard your daily utterances
While remaining committed and true.

True to that which you discern,
And to that which you know is of Me.
True to this season of consecration,
And true to your desire to be free.

Participating in intercessory prayer each week required preparation and teamwork between Kevin and me. Friday was my designated day to transport our son to school, but prayer often overlapped with that commute. I knew the seriousness of this time in prayer, so I would begin the call, pray, exit the call, prepare my son to leave, and resume the call in the car. Yet, on one particular day, my son had numerous requests while en route to school. Although I was tempted to exit the call, I heard the Holy Spirit say, "There's something for you." As I continued to listen, the Lord used Elder Sandie to describe a new season that I had entered. My transition was described as analogous to a caterpillar's metamorphosis. While returning home, God spoke.

> "But we all, with unveiled face, beholding as in a mirror the glory of the Lord, are being transformed into the same image from glory to glory, just as from the Lord, the Spirit" (2 Corinthians 3:18).

The Butterfly Effect

When a butterfly is revealed,
It is the result of unseen pain and toil.
It's the end result of confinement,
And an internal struggle and war.

Yet your revealing is quite different,
As it's marked with My hand of grace.
My anointing rests upon you—
People can see it on your face.

You've suffered and you've labored,
But in this season you have broken through.

Led by His Spirit: Spoken through Poems

Your wings are skillfully designed
To reflect this new freedom I've bestowed upon you.

Your butterfly effect is neither harsh
Nor powerful at first sight.
You'll graciously land in situations,
Deposit My anointing, and take flight.

Your beauty, though birthed from inside,
Will now gleam as the dawn of the day,
For the newness of your wing pattern and anointing
Has graced you to appear this way.

You're flying to new heights in business
And you're fluttering to see greatness in your land.
Please practice your grace and confidence
As they'll support you as you stand.

Despite the environment or circumstance,
A butterfly has her own unique effect—
You cause those who are around you
To look upward and follow the beautiful anointing you project.

Strong soul ties reach into the depths of your members. The connection is indescribable to onlookers. It simply exists and resides within a designated place in your inner self. The challenge with these relationships is their potential to preempt the role of the Holy Spirit. Without caution and discernment, the opinions, thoughts, and direction of others will usurp the authority of God's precious Holy Spirit.

> "My sheep hear My voice, and I know them, and they follow Me" (John 10:27).

A Severing of Souls

To separate is to shift
From your old dependent ways;
It's a mark of independence
And progression to a new phase.

Stop sharing every detail
And seeking each other's approval.
I'm demanding a separation
And a healthy removal.

Your decisions must be made
On what I give to you.
There's no room for soul ties
That tend to change your point of view.

You no longer fit that mold
Because I've enlightened you and set you free.

Led by His Spirit: Spoken through Poems

Stop reaching back to find
A place where you can agree.

She cannot understand your lifestyle,
For I've set you on two separate paths.
You must speedily move forward in holiness
While abandoning the pain of your past.

Your carnal conversations
Mark a place where you can always return.
But I'm removing your need for this fellowship
For it interferes with the race you must run.

You will meet again in the Spirit
And your bond will be new and revived,
For the tear that you're feeling today
Is designed to give Me increase in both of your lives.

Stephanie R. Miller

Discretion is defined as "the quality of being discreet; wise conduct and management, cautious discernment."[1]

My impulsive attempts to assist others, share my opinions, or remain connected were evidence of my need for discretion. As God continued to uproot my unbecoming character flaws, he exposed my lack of discretion.

> "As a ring of gold in a swine's snout, so is a beautiful woman who lacks discretion" (Proverbs 11:22).

Discretion

You may not do what you've done,
Nor say what you've said;
I'm tired of carnality
And the lifestyle it has bred.

You've made statements out of sheer ambiguity
And a need to be seen as "fun."
Yet, your need for the approval of others
Must be swiftly and completely undone.

For this unfamiliar land where you must travel
Requires security and confidence in My name.
It demands boldness to proclaim what I'm saying
Without question, fear, or shame.

---

1. *Webster's Collegiate Dictionary*, s.v., "discretion."

Led by His Spirit: Spoken through Poems

Don't release destructive words and comments
Into the atmosphere—
Stop extending yourself to fit in,
Because it is motivated by fear.

The fear of the Lord is the beginning of wisdom
And it's what secures your feet in My position.
The unhealthy fear of people's opinions
Will ultimately hinder your spiritual transition.

Stephanie R. Miller

I dolatry is a powerful word that describes a seemingly complicated act. As a maturing believer, I had to remain alert in the Spirit in order to reserve my worship for God alone. Without consistent self-examination, daily routines and excessive rituals have the potential to resemble acts of idolatry. When we don't completely understand that God supplies *all* our needs, we can fall prey to idolizing people and possessions.

"You shall have no other gods before Me" (Exodus 20:3).

Idolatry's Intrusion

Idolatry is false worship
Of people, symbols, or places.
It extends throughout the universe
Across color, creed, and races.

Its origin is purely satanic,
As it has no godly source.
It's created by blind allegiance,
And sustained by misuse and force.

The spirit of idolatry
Will lurk in a church, school, or home.
It plants its feet firmly
In an attempt to establish its throne.

Its initial invasion is subtle
As it may hide behind a cloak of religion.

Led by His Spirit: Spoken through Poems

It resembles true worship and prayer,
But it's tainted by obvious division.

Its followers are slowly transformed
From their God-given gifts and callings.
They're lured by the lusts of their flesh
And schemes that become enthralling.

Please don't mistake idolatry
For the honor due to My servant leaders.
An environment that is embedded with idolatry
Will soon falter under the hand of its breeder.

Stephanie R. Miller

Many believers live their lives in a constant state of guilt and/or shame. This poem was designed to usher the reader into a place of liberty and newness.

> "So if the Son makes you free, you will be free indeed"
> (John 8:36).

Be Free in Jesus' Name

Be free in Jesus' name
Be free in Jesus' name

No more guilt or pain
Be free in Jesus' name

Loose the weight of this burden and shame
Be free in Jesus' name

His victory you'll now proclaim
Be free in Jesus' name

Heartache will no longer remain
Be free in Jesus' name

Your loss is now His gain
Be free in Jesus' name

Led by His Spirit: Spoken through Poems

Washed by our Savior's blood stain
Be free in Jesus' name

Release the struggle and the strain
Be free in Jesus' name

Your life He will continually sustain
Be free in Jesus' name

Stephanie R. Miller

I heard the following words during prayer one morning: "There is no longer room for error. The time is nigh and I've not prepared you in order for you to fall prey to fear. Stand still and know that I am God."

"For God has not given us a spirit of timidity, but of power and love and discipline" (2 Timothy 1:7).

Know that I am God

When you're in the midst of turmoil,
And there's no visible means of escape,
I've trapped you in this season
So your life will change its shape.

Don't fret because of your pain,
Nor weep as if there is no hope.
Trust My hand to guide you
With a fortified spiritual rope.

There's nothing that I can't manage
For I'm the Author and Finisher of your faith.
Be steadfast and trust My guidance
As My Spirit leads you to My gate.

Once you've entered this place of intimacy,
And you trust Me with all your heart,
My Kingdom is open and free to you
To embrace a brand new start.

Led by His Spirit: Spoken through Poems

The frequency of God's poetic messages increased, and their accuracy was unfathomable. In my heart, I wanted to thank Elder Sandie for obeying the Holy Spirit's instructions. God sent her to help my spiritual progression. In this poem, God explained our reconnection and its purpose.

> "Therefore, confess your sins to one another, and pray for one another so that you may be healed. The effective prayer of a righteous man can accomplish much" (James 5:16).

The End of My Wilderness Experience

When we reconnected in the Spirit,
God sent you with a Word of Affirmation—
A Word to explain my position
And continue the process of restoration.

I was navigating through the wilderness
And seen glimpses of His marvelous light.
I was no longer trapped in darkness
Or overwhelmed by the pain of the night.

God had awakened my spiritual ears
To hear His voice as He spoke;
He had opened my tearstained eyes
To see the destruction of a lifelong yoke.

Yet, you met me at the edge of the forest,
Where the trees were beginning to thin.

Stephanie R. Miller

You shined the Light of His Anointing
To illuminate the path I'd begin.

I've walked down the path of transparency
And allowed Him to expose what I'd hidden.
I've crawled down the path of forgiveness
To address areas considered forbidden.

I've stumbled down the path of obedience
As I've struggled with the Holy Spirit as my guide.
I've jogged down the path of intercession
Attempting to pray by His side.

Now I'm stomping down the path of warfare,
For I'm determined to fight for what I see.
I thank you for leading this stampede
And awakening the warrior in me.

Led by His Spirit: Spoken through Poems

As I sought God's face daily and awaited manna, my faith was elevated. Spiritually, I could see and hear differently, but naturally, I was uncertain about what God truly desired for me.

> "'For I know the plans that I have for you,' declares the Lord, 'plans for welfare and not for calamity to give you a future and a hope'" (Jeremiah 29:11).

An Anointed Return

Do not be dismayed
By the voices that you hear—
The folks who try to tell you
To remain in a place of fear.

The enemy can see you moving
To a place of obedience and trust.
He's employing every tactic
Because your demise is a must.

The degree of your true anointing
Has not been released for all to see.
It's hidden and divinely protected
Until the day when you must decree.

You'll decree to those around you
Of My ability to prepare you for this season.
You'll decree to those who question you

Stephanie R. Miller

That I've granted you discernment and reason.

Don't take it lightly that I speak to you,
For your environment tends to believe otherwise.
I'm here for those who seek Me
And are striving for the ultimate prize.

Stand guard and uphold your position
For your strategy is to exude My joy.
You'll illuminate places of darkness
To shine before every man, woman, girl, and boy.

This is a season of deliverance
And a time to set the captive free.
My anointing will flow freely
And loose many to return to Me.

Led by His Spirit: Spoken through Poems

Just as I was leaving my prayer closet one evening, Barbara called. She made a very specific prayer request regarding a financial need. She shared that her church was praying and fasting using the 9th chapter of Job as their focus.

"Who does great things, unfathomable, and wondrous works without number" (Job 9:10).

Beyond Numbers

A number is a limit to the amount that I can do
A number is a boundary that prevents you from breaking through

A number stifles your vision and disables spiritual progression
A number binds My children and sends their minds into recession

A number hinders your potential as it presents a finite goal
A number thrusts you into an incomprehensible role

My children can never measure My blessings from on high
My works are unfathomable to the onlooker's ear or eye

When you call I have already answered and made provision for your need
My omnipotence equates My wondrous works and overshadows your tendency toward greed

I started the first day of a twenty-one day fast and while reading the focus Scriptures, I turned to the 2nd chapter of Luke. This chapter describes the character of God's faithful servant, Anna.

> "She never left the temple, serving night and day with fasting and prayers" (Luke 2:37b).

Where is Anna?

Does Anna still sit in My temple on her knees
Patiently waiting to worship, pray, and please

Her Father in heaven who has redeemed and set her free?
Anna understands that her life belongs to Me.

She's a daughter in My kingdom that has received her heavenly call;
She's risen to the occasion and sees victory through it all.

Her hands are committed to war as she prays in My temple.
Her ears are finely tuned and she speaks words that are wise and simple.

Anna knows My voice so that she's not easily distracted—
Her consecrated lifestyle prevents our fellowship from being infracted.

My cousin, Patrice, was celebrating her fortieth birthday on a February 8th. In honor of this blessed occasion, her husband planned a surprise party. These words of exhortation were given for her.

> "The thief comes only to steal and kill and destroy; I came that they may have life, and have it abundantly" (John 10:10).

Forty Years Full

Forty years full of joy.

Forty years full of delight.

Forty years of challenging anything that wasn't quite right.

Forty years of unmatched humor.

Forty years of unique expression.

Forty years of forward movement with minimal regression.

Forty years of unseen challenges.

Forty years of love and compassion.

Forty years of serving with great satisfaction.

Forty years of traits from your mother.

Forty years of traits from your daddy.

Forty years of assuming the mantle of your Grandmother, Hattie.

Over the last forty years God has perfected a work in you.

He has used your voice of intercession to invoke, release, and push through.

Stephanie R. Miller

He has established your very footsteps and enabled you to reach;
He has called you by name and anointed you to preach.

Our Father has great plans for a future and a hope,
But in order to reach this level you must spiritually elope.

Take refuge in Our Father and seclude yourself with Him.
Our Healer and our Comforter will inhabit a new place within.

Don't doubt Him because of your wounds,
Don't reject Him because of your loss,
Our Father is coming to restore you by the blood of our Savior's cross.

So as you embark upon the blessed age of forty!
Take delight in this one thing:
Jesus already bore your pain and eradicated any residual sting.

Led by His Spirit: Spoken through Poems

Each time the Holy Spirit led me to write another poem, I wondered how this book would end. God spoke fervently and with such comfort that I believed what He was showing me. On the seventh day of my twenty-one day fast, the Holy Spirit spoke two words at the end of this poem. Those words were "THE END."

> "The Lord said, 'I have surely seen the affliction of My people who are in Egypt, and have given heed to their cry because of their taskmasters, for I am aware of their sufferings. So I have come down to deliver them from the power of the Egyptians, and to bring them up from that land to a good and spacious land, to a land flowing with milk and honey'" (Exodus 3:7-8).

A New Land

You're complete and lacking nothing,
As My hand has ushered you through.
As Moses led the Israelites,
Child, I predestined to lead you too.

Led you through great pain and anger,
Led you through sickness and depression,
Led you through years that were confusing,
But were a catalyst for spiritual progression.

The wilderness has unique benefits
For My children who survive the unforeseen.
They're prepared for natural disasters
With the covering of My Holy brigandine.

Stephanie R. Miller

Their hands are divinely equipped for battle
As they understand both spiritual and natural war.
Though they moan and complain while in transition,
They're unable to return to their lives from before.

My sons and daughters have fought many
As they've traveled from land to land.
They've abandoned every natural weight or harness
That would inhibit their ability to stand.

So rejoice as you've reached your promise!
Stand still and observe what I've done!
Your wilderness experience has ended,
And the battle you have definitely won.

Take possession of that which I will show you,
For I've set aside this great land just for you.
Walk confidently into the light of My exposure
That will establish a new life for you.

"But you are a chosen race, a royal priesthood, a holy nation, a people for God's own possession, so that you may proclaim the excellencies of Him who has called you out of darkness into His marvelous light" (1 Peter 2:9).

About the Author

Stephanie has worked as a licensed and certified speech-language pathologist for more than nineteen years. She and her husband, Kevin, have been married for fourteen. The Millers reside in Cleveland, Ohio with their eight-year-old son, Justin.

To contact Stephanie e-mail: speak2teach@email.com

More Titles by 5 Fold Media

The Transformed Life
by John R. Carter
$20.95
ISBN: 978-1-936578-40-5

Personal transformation requires radical change, but your life will not transform until you change the way you think. Becoming a Christian ignites the process of transformation.

In this book, John Carter will teach you that God has designed a plan of genuine transformation for every person, one that goes far beyond the initial moment of salvation. More than a book, this 10 week, 40 day workbook will show you how to change.

Letters from Heaven
The Passion Translation
by Brian Simmons
$12.95
ISBN: 978-1-936578-56-6

Some of the most beautiful and glorious truths of the Bible are found in the letters of the Apostle Paul. Paul's letters are now available in The Passion Translation. Reading through these letters is like having Paul sitting in your living room personally sharing his experience of the power and majesty of God's Word for His people. Be ready to sense the stirring of the Holy Spirit within you as you read Letters from Heaven by the Apostle Paul.

I highly recommend this new Bible translation to everyone.
~ Dr. Ché Ahn, Senior Pastor of HRock Church in Pasadena, CA

Like 5 Fold Media on Facebook, follow us on Twitter!

"To Establish and Reveal"
For more information visit:
www.5foldmedia.com

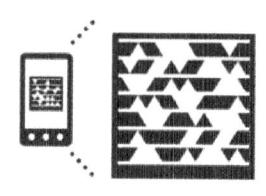

Use your mobile device to scan the tag above and visit our website.
Get the free app:
http://gettag.mobi

CPSIA information can be obtained at www.ICGtesting.com
Printed in the USA
BVOW08s0408140714

359090BV00005B/19/P